Mom, Me and Magic

Divya Venkatesan

BookLeaf Publishing

India | USA | UK

Mom, Me and Magic © 2024 Divya Venkatesan

All rights reserved.

No part of this publication may be reproduced, stored in a retrieval system, or transmitted, in any form or by any means, electronic, mechanical, photocopying, recording or otherwise, without the prior written permission of the presenters.

Divya Venkatesan asserts the moral right to be identified as author of this work.

Presentation by *BookLeaf Publishing*

Web: www.bookleafpub.com

E-mail: info@bookleafpub.com

ISBN: 9789363316997

First edition 2024

This book is dedicated to my mom, who introduced me to the world of books, my son, whose actions were the source of my inspiration and the late author Enid Blyton, an epitome of brilliance and creativity and my prime role model in the world of children's fantasy books.

ACKNOWLEDGEMENT

To my readers. Amidst your busy schedules, thank you for making the effort to order and choose to read this book. It means a lot.

To my closest family and friends. I know I could count on you at all times. Thank you for backing me during this journey and allowing me the space and time to complete this book successfully. I hope I have made you proud.

To my blogger group. Ladies! The kind of support and encouragement that I received, from day one of joining the group, to date has been immense. Thank you for inspiring me and instilling confidence to take my work to the next level. This book is yours, as much as mine.

To this world with different things, different people, different lifestyles and many more. You have given me so much content to write about.

To Instagram. Insta, you instantly won over my regards by popping up the advertisement regarding the BookLeaf Publishing writer challenge. If not for your insistence, this work would have been one of those many lines hidden in mobile notes.

To my publisher. I would like to immensely thank BookLeaf Publishing for The Write Angle Challenge, which instigated and provided me with this wonderful opportunity to make my dream of publishing my work come true. A special thanks to my entire publishing team for their constant support and guidance, which helped turn this work into something more wonderful.

Finally, to God, I am forever grateful.

PREFACE

There may be no dearth to the number of poetry books available. But, what makes this book special is that it is written by a mother from the perspective of her child.

How would the child think in different environments? How would the child react or feel to different situations? As a mother, it is definitely intriguing and on some occasions challenging to guess their reactions, but the suspense element is what makes life with them colorful.

There is no bond that is more special for a mother than the one she shares with her child. As for the child, their mom is their whole world until they learn about the world through her.

This book has been one of my most cherished experiences. It is a humble attempt to pen down about that magical connection and the tales of mischief and magic in the most purest and simple form.

It can be read to children, read with them and read by them to you. If it ticks it all, that would be the success intended.

I hope you enjoy the magic just as I did!

Index

Red ant 1

What should I carry? 2

Feel fine! 4

Housefly 6

Bathroom saga 7

Save the sparrow 9

What do I like? 11

That Trigger Word. 12

Once upon a time… 13

Share and play. 15

Mischief manageable? 16

Smile in sleep 18

Favorite pastimes 19

It is magical 21

Curious me 23

What is Ah-ju-ya? 25

Moments of magic 28

What should I do when I grow old? 30

Red ant

I followed a red ant
In my little baggy pant
It was carrying sand
In its teeny-tiny hand.

I wondered where it went
Oh! The floor had a sudden dent
I bowed down with my knees bent
To see it building its winter tent.

Up. Up. I hear them say
It was a very sunny day
Move across and make way
For they were busy storing food and hay.

I thought to help a bit
Brought them pieces of my favorite biscuit
Out came a big fleet
Carrying along the food for its winter needs.

What should I carry?

What should I carry?
That was my biggest worry.

There is the pink doll 'Curly'
With bright blue eyes smiling merrily.
Hurriedly as I picked,
I saw the others left behind.

Guddu the bear
Or Bunny the hare.
Creamy the camel
Or my favorite noisy vessel.
What should I carry?
That was my biggest worry.

Rum, rum truck
Or the squeaky yellow duck.
Oh! There are so many more,
How can I leave those balls on the floor!
What should I carry?
That was my biggest worry.

Mom told me to hurry
We were going to pick cherry
Traveling on a ferry
With my cousin Terry.

What toy should I carry?
During that entire journey,
That was my biggest worry.

Feel fine!

Woke up from my sleep
Didn't find my mom next to me!
Should I start to cry?
Or search all sides for a while?

I don't know how to call.
Crying is my only shot.
Should I crawl out to the hall?
Oh! Why am I alone on the cot?

I feel so scared.
Mom, are you here?
I can't see you yet
Though I can feel your breath.

Her face emerged above mine.
It was such a happy sign.
She was here all the time.
Now, I feel very fine.

Housefly

I saw a big housefly
Sitting on the tube light
Flapping its wings,
But disappeared in a blink.

Zzz. Zzz. I hear the sound
I eagerly look around.
It's back before my eyes
Oh, it's definitely huge in size.

I stretch my hand to catch
It kept flying so fast
It was a good pastime
Trying to catch a big housefly.

Bathroom saga

My mom went to take a bath.
I started to cry so hard.
I could hear her through the door
But I could not see her anymore.

How could she leave me out?
So I thought it's time to shout.

Let me bang on that door.
Or should I try rolling on the floor?
What will make her come out soon?
I can't wait to see her back in the room.

How could she leave me out?
Let me cry a little more aloud.

Momma, momma, I call out to her.
Can she hear, or should I be more clear?
Papa, Dadda, Granny all are here,
But all I want is my mom near.

Finally, I hear the door opening sound.
Instantly making me smile as I see her coming
out.

Save the sparrow

Out through the window
I saw a house sparrow
Sitting on the wire fence
Making sounds pretty dense.

I thought it was calling me
So I went out to see,
What it needs.

A thorn stuck in its leg
It was getting hard to stretch
I knew it was asking for help
That made my heart melt.

I didn't know what to do
The sky was turning dark blue
How do I remove it without getting hurt?
That was the only thought that I had.

I called my friends around
We spotted the ladder on ground
Slowly but tightly, we held the sparrow
To remove the thorn and let it fly without any
sorrow.

What do I like?

I like to run
I like to throw
It's magical to see the toys on the floor.

My mom came around
With food in a bowl,
Now I like to flip and roll.

Carrot or beans
Apple or greens
I like to reject before I even eat

Cause babies have a common ground
We like to throw tantrums
For reasons just unknown.

That Trigger Word.

Tata! Bye.
Yes, I heard that word right.
You can't do anything now
Without taking me out.

Isn't there a lot to see?
Cars on the road with big wheels.
I'm so happy and excited.
So, just get up from your seat.

My thoughts are on the crow
I hear it cawing far above.
Let's go out to see,
I can't contain my glee.

You might wonder what is the hurry
But the word 'bye' triggered all merry
It's time to go out immediately
Or what I might miss, is my real worry.

Once upon a time…

Here's my favorite
'Once upon a time' tale.
Hope you like it
Let's go hear it.

Once upon a time, there lived a big mouse.
Ki. Ki. Ki.
Say, Ki. Ki. Ki.

Every day it used to go, search for cheese.
Cheese cheese cheese.
Say, cheese cheese cheese.

But there lived a cat, right across the street.
Street, street, street.
Right across the street.

The cat chased the rat.
Ra-ta-ta-ta-tat. Ra-ta-ta-ta-tat.
The rat got scared.

The rat got scared.
It ran into a hole.
Deep deep down.
Krr. Krr. Krr.
Krr. Krr. Krr.
Making it its new home.

Share and play.

My cousin Terry came home
We went up to see the moon.
He is just a little older than me,
But different from all the adults I see.

Out came the sun
We began to run.
I liked what he held
So I grabbed it from his hand.

Mom told me to share.
That's how you play fair.
Aren't you a naughty boy?
But I cried; it's my toy.

Terry went back home
There was no one to play with anymore.
I decided to share and play,
Cause that's when there's a lot of joy.

Mischief manageable?

I fell on the floor
And hurt my elbow.
Does this stop me?
No, I'm very naughty.

Tear the paper,
Pour the water,
Pull the curtain,
These have no end.
I'm busy the whole day
Creating mess all my way.

Expect the unexpected
Even then, it's difficult
Cause nothing shall stop me
From being naughty.

Can you guess,
What will I do next?
Ha ha, that's my little secret.

Smile in sleep

She said I smiled while I slept
It's due to all those things that I dreamt.

Cows and sheep came to graze
I ran free through the green maze.
It's so happy to watch them
That I shouted moo and baa in tandem.

Lots of sweets
Filled with ghee.
Shop with toys
Making merry noises.
I dream of these
In my sleep
Which brings that smile
On my face.

Favorite pastimes

Step on grandma's shoes
Which covers only my toes.
Pick up a dirty vase
And lick it immediately to taste.

Spot any waste on the floor
Fiddle with it to find what's in store
Scribble except on paper
As art feels like my superpower.

Snuggle baby Jumbo elephant
Blabber words loud and chant.
Spread toys in every corner
But never let anyone move it further.

My naughty pastimes are so many
But I can't reveal everything to you
Cause these are secrets of mine
To ensure my mom's attention is just on me.

It is magical

Water from tap
To that woolen monkey cap.
Birds that fly so high
To a horse's neigh.
Dog that walked past me
To the buzzing honey bee.
Every little thing
Is fascinating.

Bells in temples
To a glass full of pickles.
Colorful bouncing balls
To dancing little dolls.
Bangles that you wear
To papers that I tear.
Every little thing
Is so fascinating.

Sun rays seeping through the windows
To cattle's grazing in the meadows.
The chairs with four legs
To items-filled dad's office desk.
There's so much to know
That makes my face smile and glow
Every little thing
Is just so fascinating.

Mom, this world is like a wonder.
It may seem simpler.
But, in my eyes
It's all magical.

Curious me

What are they?
How to play?
Is this real?
Why to gargle?
Questions are many.
Oh, shall I bathe my Bunny?

Where to keep?
Why should I sleep.?
Whose shoe is that?
When will the sun set?
Who will answer?
Do they know it well?

Which ice cream to choose?
Can we play in the pool?
Whom should I ask?
Isn't that my mask?
Did you give it to her?
Have you got any flowers?

I have too many questions to ask.
Are you prepared for that task?
This is curious little me
Answer me, please.

What is Ah-ju-ya?

One afternoon
We sat in our drawing room,
Busily sketching mountains, trees
And tiny little houses.

I held out my hand and said Ah-ju-ya
My mom asked me who was 'Ambuja'?!

That evening, I was with grandpa
Watering the plants in our garden.
As water splashed on the leaves
A sudden thought struck through me.

I held out my hand and said Ah-ju-ya
Grandpa asked, do you want papaya?!

Tired and hungry,
I went to the kitchen
To fill my tummy.
I held my hand out to grandma.
She gave me a peeled banana.

I cry out Ah-ju-ya
She made me some Semiya!

Dad came home from work
Carrying his black laptop bag.
Switched on the television
To watch India batting, live-action.

I ran to him and said Ah-ju-ya.
He boasts thinking, I said Tendulkar.

Late at night, cousin Terry came home.
He was talking on the cordless phone.
I sprint to him and said Ah-ju-ya
He handed me the phone in hand.

Happily, I danced around
As someone got my Ah-ju-ya.
All I meant was give it to me,
But everyone understood it differently.

I thought I said my words clear
Why don't they just understand?
Soon I will talk like them
Until then, it's going to be some fun.

Moments of magic

The first time I hugged my mom
The first time I played with dad
The first time I flipped over
The first time I crawled under
Words cannot define
Such moments of magic.

The first time I walked
The first time I had a great fall
The first time I saw the moon
The first time I entered my room
Words cannot define
Such moments of magic.

The first time I said a word
The first time I saw a bird
The first time I went to park
The first time I heard 'baby shark'
Words cannot define
Such moments of magic.

The first time I opened a box
The first time I saw a real fox
The first time I sang a song
The first time I wrote on a wall
Words cannot define
Such moments of magic.

For every one of my first,
Mom, dad and everyone happily fussed
But words cannot define
Such moments of magic.

What should I do when I grow old?

What should I do?
When I grow old.

Astrology to begin with,
Bird watching across the vast width.
Cooking like an explorer,
Dancing until you disappear.
Embroidery to display,
Fishkeeping to just play.
Garden to charm,
Hiking to transform.
Instagramming the new way,
Journaling about the entire day.
Karate to secure a belt,
Laze around and just be dealt.
Music to maneuver,
Nature walk in Vancouver.

Online shopping, a killer best,
Painting, to feel and express.
Quilling is the art in town,
Reading, to not let the legacy down.
Sports is all to think about,
Travel the world without any doubt.
Uno as a favorite pastime,
Video gaming past bedtime.
Wrestling way through real hard,
X-Men, Avengers are true fan wars.
YouTube to distract,
Zoom calls to hold your back.

Mom gave me an A to Z list
For now, I'm just going to take rest
And do what I do best,
Play, fuss and create a lot of naughty mess.

www.ingramcontent.com/pod-product-compliance
Lightning Source LLC
LaVergne TN
LVHW010922200726
843509LV00013B/2029